THE THINGS WE USE

Published by Raintree Steck-Vaughn Publishers, an imprint of Steck-Vaughn Company.

Library of Congress Cataloging-in-Publication Data

Hewitt, Sally.
　　　　The things we use / Sally Hewitt and Jane Rowe.
　　　　　　　　p.　　　cm. —(Have You Noticed?)
　　　　Includes index.
　　　　Summary:　Examines the function, design, and technology of such everyday things as eating utensils, chairs, and telephones.
　　　　　　　ISBN　0-8172-4601-0
　　　　1. Technology—Miscellanea — Juvenile literature.　　　2. Inventions—Miscellanea—Juvenile literature　　　　　3. Design, Industrial—Miscellanea—Juvenile Literature　　(1. Technology. 2. Inventions.)　　I. Rowe, Jane.　II. Title　III. Series.
T48.H38　1997
670—dc20　　　　　　　　　　　　　　　　　96-34733
　　　　　　　　　　　　　　　　　　　　　　　　　CIP
　　　　　　　　　　　　　　　　　　　　　　　　　AC

Printed in Spain
Bound in the United States
1 2 3 4 5 6 7 8 9 0 LB 02 01 00 99 98 97 96

Acknowledgments

Editorial: Ann Kay, Heather Luff
Design: Ann Samuel
Production: Jenny Mulvanny
Photography: Michael Stannard, except for the following:

Page 12: deckchair (Last Resort Picture Library), office chair (Wallis Office Furniture, Essex); page 13: dentist's chair (Sempre/Harri Kosonen/Cottrell & Co.); page 17: trolley (Capital Links Ltd, London); page 22: baby buggy (Mothercare), suitcase (Samsonite), wheelchair (Invacare/Carters Ltd, Mid-Glamorgan); page 26: baby's cot (Mothercare); page 27: bedroom scene (Last Resort Picture Library), headrest (British Museum); page 28: chair (Ron Arad, London/photo Christoph Kicherer), toast rack (designer: Marie Fesowicz-Smith/The New Designers Exhibition at the Business Design Centre, London); page 29: citrus juicer (Philippe Starck/Alessi).

Thanks also to:
Hutchinson Children's publishers for permission to show the book *Old Bear*, by Jane Hissey (page 6); Habitat for permission to use their catalogue in the collage on page 13; our models Marie Attwood (cover, pages 12, 20); Michelle Man (pages 7, 10, 21); Amy Weeks (pages 8 and 9); Danny Butt (page 18); Rosie Crews (pages 10 and 21).

Artworks and models:
Sue Woollatt/Graham-Cameron Illustration agency (border artworks on cover and inside and phone a/ws page 20); Jenny Crowe (mugs on page 7); the pupils of Christchurch Primary School, Bristol (posters on page 15); Claudia Pagliarani (chair collage page 13 and folders page 19); Bev Knowlden (truck on page 23).

Have You Noticed?

THE
THINGS
WE USE

Sally Hewitt and Jane Rowe

RSVP
RAINTREE
STECK-VAUGHN
PUBLISHERS
The Steck Vaughn Company

Austin, Texas

About This Book

This book has been put together in a way that makes it ideal for parents to share with their young children. Take time with each question and project and have fun learning about how all sorts of different objects have been designed for a special purpose.

The Things We Use deals with some ideas about design and technology that many children will be exposed to as they play. The pictures and text will encourage children to explore design on the page as well as all around them. This will help them to understand why objects are a certain shape, why they are made from particular materials, and why they work well and are easy to use. It will also help them to develop their own design skills.

The "Eye-opener" boxes reveal interesting and unusual facts, or lead children to examine one particular aspect of design. There are also projects that put theory into practice in an entertaining and informative way. Children learn most effectively by joining in, talking, asking questions, and solving problems. So encourage them to talk about what they are doing and to find ways of solving the problems for themselves.

Try to make thinking about design and technology a part of everyday life. Just pick up any object around the house and talk about why it has been made that way, and how it could be improved. Design is not just a subject for adults. You can have a lot of fun with it at any age — and develop both artistic flair and practical skills.

Contents

The Things We Use

What do you do every day?
You are probably busy from morning to night.

Here are some things you might use each day.

What else do you use?

The people who decide how things are made
are called designers.

They try to design things so that they do their job well,
are safe to use, and look attractive.

For example a
well-designed mug
has to hold hot and
cold drinks.

It should not break easily.
It must have a strong handle.

What else must it have
in order to work well?

▼ The designer of the mugs
below has made some
mistakes.

Can you see what
they are?

This book will tell you about the design of
some of the things we use every day.

In the Kitchen

A kitchen must be clean and safe because that is where food is cooked and stored.

▶To keep your hands clean, you use your foot to push the pedal on a garbage can full of trash.

▲ Rubber gloves protect your hands when you are washing dishes and cleaning the kitchen.

▲Oven mitts are made of thick material so you can hold hot dishes without burning yourself.

◀When the sharp blades of these knives are placed into a knife block, nobody can cut themselves by mistake.

Kitchens are full of objects that are designed to do special jobs.

A rolling pin is just the right shape for rolling out pastry.

▼ Look at this picture carefully. Can you tell what each object has been used for?

Eating and Drinking

You could use your hands to eat and drink, but they would get very messy. Hot food and drink also would burn them.

Instead we use plates, bowls, cups, and utensils.

Do you think that all the objects on these pages have been well-designed to do their job?

▲ A fork is used to hold food steady while the sharp knife is used to cut off a bite-sized piece.

◀ Chopsticks are useful for picking up small chunks of food and scooping up mouthfuls of rice and noodles.

Which pieces of flatware
and dinnerware would a person
need to eat this meal?
Don't forget to pick
a serving spoon, too.

Sitting Comfortably

Look at the shape Susan's body makes when she is sitting down. It fits the shape of the chair like a puzzle piece.

Chairs should be designed to give our bodies comfortable support whatever we are doing.

▼ What would you be doing if you were sitting on one of these chairs?

The objects shown next to the chairs give you a clue.

A dentist's chair is adjustable.
The dentist can move it up and down and change its shape.

Look for some other adjustable chairs on these two pages.

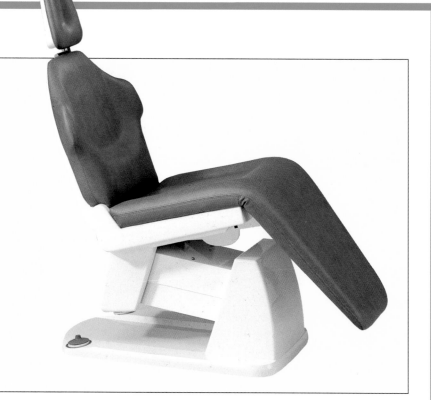

Make a collage

Cut out pictures of chairs from magazines and newspapers to make your own collage. Look at all the different shapes and materials the designers have chosen.

Writing, Drawing, and Painting

We have pens and pencils for writing and drawing.
We have brushes and rollers for painting.
How well do they do their job?

◀ A pencil is long and thin so that your fingers can easily hold it to draw and to write.

◀ Try writing your name holding a pencil the way you would hold a paint roller.

How would you hold each of these different pens, pencils, and brushes?
What would you use each one for?

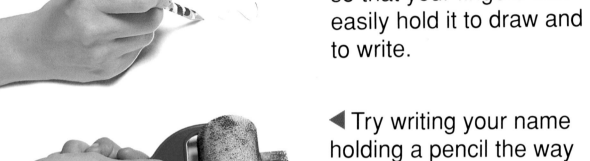

Design a poster

Do you think these are
good posters for
a fair?

Try designing a poster for
yourself or for a school play.

Your poster must have all
the important information on it.
It must make people stop and look.
It also must be easy to read.

Sketch your poster in pencil first,
so that you can change your ideas
and correct mistakes.

EYE-OPENER

Which of these two pencil sharpeners
do you think works better?
Think about how to hold them.
Think about what happens to
the shavings.
Would they both fit into your pencil case?

Which one would you rather use?

Stacking and Storing

Mary has a very small bedroom. Look how much space her things are taking up!

Now Mary has put her things in crates. The crates stack on top of each other. Look how little space Mary's things take up now.

EYE-OPENER

Cones are a good shape for stacking. Look for different cone-shaped objects that can be stacked like these.

Storage carts like this come in many different sizes.

What could you keep in a small cart that looked like this? What could you keep in a large one?

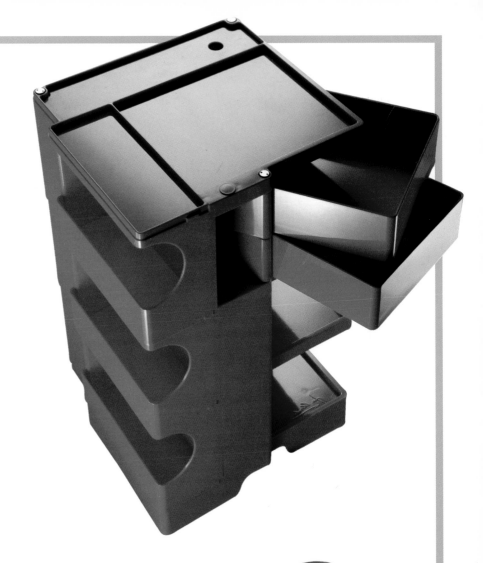

A desk organizer is designed to store all kinds of things.

Will everything here fit into this desk organizer?

Carrying

What would happen if you tried to carry all this to school without a bag? It might rain, you could drop something, and your arms would probably hurt.

▼ This backpack lets you carry your things comfortably and leaves your hands free.

What kind of bag would you choose to carry your things to school?

Design a folder

Do you have drawings or notes that need to be carried to school? Why not make your own folder from cardboard to do the job?

1. Measure the largest piece of paper you want to put in the folder so that you know how big your folder must be.

2. Draw a plan in pencil on the cardboard as shown.

3. Carefully cut out the folder along the solid lines.

4. Fold along the dotted lines. Keep the lines on the outside of the folder so that you can see them. Erase the lines when you have finished folding.

5. Glue the pieces together at the sides.

6. Decorate your folder in any way you like.

Telephones

A telephone is designed to be used by four parts of your body — your ear that listens, your mouth that speaks, your hand that holds it, and your finger that dials.

Why would these strange-looking telephones be difficult to use?

EYE-OPENER

The numbers on a telephone are always placed in this order. The number 5 often has one or two raised bumps on or near it to help blind people dial.

If your telephone has a bump, try using it to help you find the other numbers with your eyes closed.

20

▶You need both hands to use this heavy, old-fashioned phone.

▲This telephone has a screen so that you can see the person you are talking to.

▲You can carry this mobile phone around in your pocket.

◀What animal do you think this strange telephone is supposed to look like?

Now try designing a phone that you would like to use.

On Wheels

You can see wheels everywhere, all specially designed to do their job

▶ The wheels on this baby carriage swivel in all directions so that it can be moved around in awkward places.

◀ Why is it easier to pull this heavy suitcase along on wheels than it is to lift it?

▶ If you used a wheelchair, how easy would your trip to school be?

Look for automatic doors, ramps, and other things that might help wheelchair users.

Make a truck with wheels that turn

Wheels turn on a rod, which is called an axle. Test this out for yourself by making this truck.

You will need:

A small box
1 or 2 drinking straws
Cardboard
Modeling clay
Scissors

1. Cut a truck shape out of your box as shown.

2. Get an adult to help you push a hole through each triangle shape with scissors.

3. Cut 4 wheels out of your cardboard. Make a hole in the middle of each one.

4. Cut your straws to make two axles that are wider than your truck. Push them through the holes in the triangles and put a wheel and a ball of modeling clay on each end.

5. Think of ways to decorate your truck.

What happens if you put square or triangular wheels on your truck?

Washing and Scrubbing

Is your bathroom full of all kinds of things to help keep you clean from head to toe?

▶ These brushes are the right size and shape to clean different parts of your body.

Why does the back brush have a long handle?

Could you clean your teeth with the nailbrush?

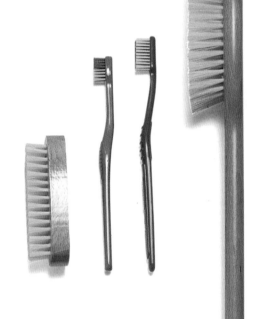

▶ All these things are useful for washing yourself.
Look out for wash-cloths and sponges of all colors, materials, shapes, and sizes.

What makes you choose a soap?
Is it the soap's
shape, size,
color, or smell?

EYE-OPENER

When you travel you don't want everything in your toiletry bag to get wet and soapy.

All your wash things can be kept clean and dry in this toiletry bag. Can you see how?

Can you find something wrong in this box? The answer is on page 32.

Bedtime

The beds on this page are designed for people sleeping in different places.

▶A baby sleeps in a crib like this. Cribs keep babies from rolling out of bed while they are asleep.

A sleeping bag is designed to be packed away so that it can be stored and carried easily.

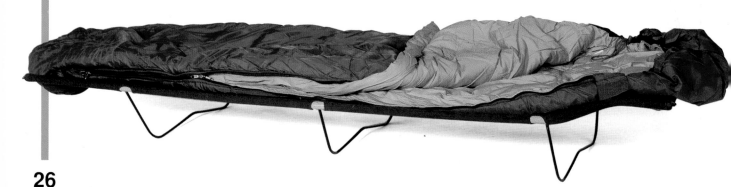

How many different kinds of material can you see in this bedroom?

Feel your pillow, mattress, and blankets.
What do they feel like?
Do you know what material they are made of?
Why do you think they are made of that material?

EYE-OPENER

You probably use a soft pillow.

In some places people prefer stone headrests like the ancient one shown here.

Amazing Designs

Each one of these objects does an ordinary, everyday job. But look how imaginative the designers have been with colors, shapes, and materials.

How easily can you tell what each object is for?

If you are not sure, the answers are on page 32.

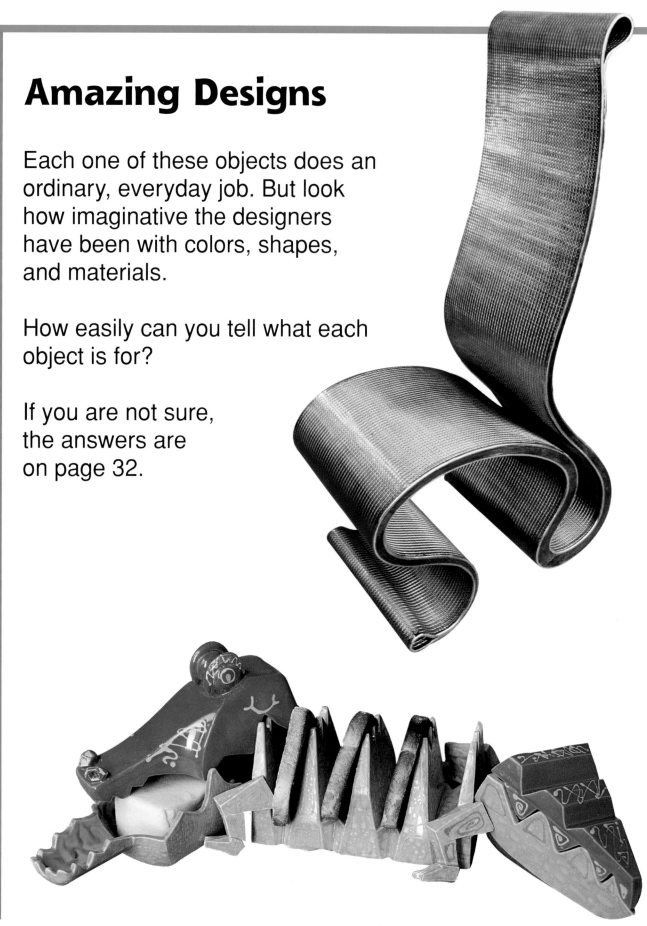

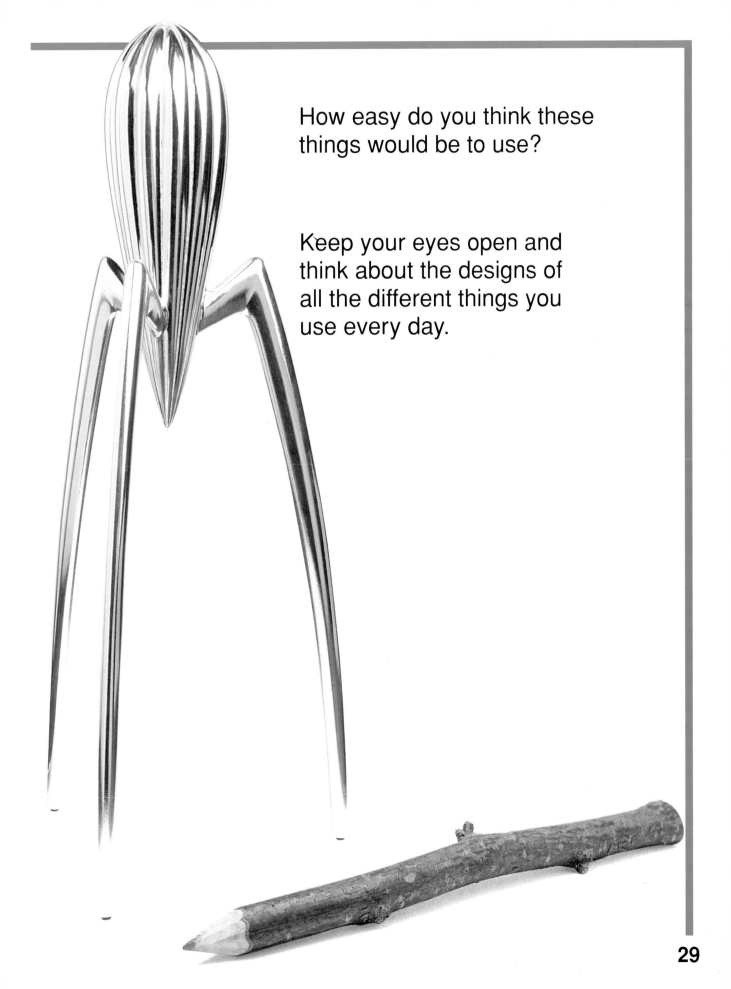

How easy do you think these things would be to use?

Keep your eyes open and think about the designs of all the different things you use every day.

? Think About...

Here are some questions to see what you have learned about the things we use. Read each question and see if you can answer it.

If you can't find the answers check the bottom of page 31.

1. Bicycles
   ◆ Three parts of a bicycle have been specially made for three different parts of your body to use. What are they?

2. Fingertips
   ◆ Can you name some things that have been specially designed for your fingertips?

3. Hands
   ◆ Can you name some things that have been specially designed to be held by your hand?

4. Juice pitchers
   ◆ A juice pitcher has been designed to hold and pour juice. What parts of the pitcher have been specially designed to do that job?

5. Specially made things
   ◆ What are a vase and a plate designed for?

6. Things without jobs
   - ◆ Can you find some things in your house that look attractive but have no special job?

7. What things are made of
   - ◆ Everything is made of some sort of material. Find a teaspoon, a rolling pin, and a comb. What are they made of?

8. Things that are flat
   - ◆ Why are a table top, a bed, and a chopping board all flat?

9. Things that are metal
   - ◆ Why are pots and pans made of metal?

10. Chairs
   - ◆ Chairs can look very different. What is the one thing that must be the same about every chair?

ANSWERS: 1. seat — to sit on, handlebars — for your hands to hold, pedals — for your feet to push 2. Telephone buttons, light switches, and computer keyboards 3. Pens, pencils, hairbrush handles, toothbrushes, flatware, and mug handles 4. A lip — to pour, a space — to hold the juice, and a handle — to pick it up 5. A vase — to hold water and flowers, a plate — to serve food 6. Any kind of ornaments 7. A teaspoon — metal or plastic, a rolling pin —wood or marble, a comb — plastic, metal, or wood 8. So that the things you place on them do not slide off 9. Metal does not melt or burn easily 10. You must be able to sit on it.

Index

Answers to pages 25, 28, and 29:

Page 25: The soap is not the same shape as the soap dish.

Page 28: A chair (top) and a toast rack (bottom). What is in the animal's jaws?

Page 29: (Top) A juicer for getting the juice from fruit such as lemons. (How would you collect the juice?). (Bottom) A colored pencil disguised as a twig of a tree.